Kitchen Table Theology

Kitchen Table Theology

Wisdom from the Heart and Hearth

by Peg Stokman

Saint Mary's Press
Christian Brothers Publications
Winona, Minnesota

To my grandchildren,
who are teaching me how
to be small enough to see God.

The publishing team included Carl Koch, development
editor; Laurie Berg Rohda, manuscript editor; Amy
Schlumpf Manion, typesetter; Maurine R. Twait, art
director; inside illustrations by Clare vanBrandwijk;
cover photo by Leigh Charlton; pre-press, printing, and
binding by the graphics division of Saint Mary's Press.

The psalms in this book are from *Psalms Anew: In
Inclusive Language,* compiled by Nancy Schreck and
Maureen Leach (Winona, MN: Saint Mary's Press, 1986).
Copyright © 1986 by Saint Mary's Press. All rights
reserved.

The scriptural material on page 20 is freely adapted
and is not to be understood or used as an official translation of the Bible.

The acknowledgments continue on page 119.

Printed in the United States of America

Printing: 9 8 7 6 5 4 3 2 1

Year: 2004 03 02 01 00 99 98 97 96

ISBN 0-88489-378-2

 Genuine recycled paper with 10% post-consumer
waste. Printed with soy-based ink.

Preface

I am a prairie theologian, discovering God incarnated in the ordinariness of life. My occupation is that of a spiritual seeker, a lover of nature, family, and friends, a minister of healing, and a writer.

Faith for me is incarnational, rooted in the experience of life. I attempt to live with my eyes wide open, looking for fresh nuances of God's presence as I worship, read scripture, interact with my family, play with my grandchildren, walk in nature, and minister to others.

I am overjoyed to have Saint Mary's Press as my publisher because the inspiration for these columns came early one morning, across the campus from Saint Mary's Press, at Saint Mary's University in Winona, Minnesota. I was in a small dorm room during a graduate school summer session. As I poured out my deep gratitude to God for the privilege of being back in school after thirty-five years, I did not expect a response. But I got one: share my new learnings and experiences of God in short reflections in a column for our diocesan newspaper.

Fr. Bill Graham, my liturgy professor that summer, described a friend's awareness of God in her everyday life as "kitchen table theology." When I heard him say that, I knew that I had my title. The editors back home accepted my proposal, and for four years now, I have enjoyed communicating weekly with the readers of the *West Nebraska Register.* I share my discoveries in a style that I hope is succinct, heart-centered, and faith-filled.

Praying These Reflections

As busy people we often want to pray, but do not think that we have the time. With this in mind, I wrote the reflections in this book. They may be used in order or randomly. Use them as you need them. Even if you just have time to read a reflection quickly, do so. Each reflection plants a seed of faith in our heart. God, our good intentions, and a little attentiveness can nourish the seed and help it grow.

One reflection pondered throughout the day becomes a day of prayer. The book might be kept in a purse, desk, or glove compartment. The reflections can provide a brief, midday connection with God during the many periods of waiting in our life: before a doctor's appointment, during car repairs, or on a coffee break.

When a longer period is available, expand your reflection by journaling, by offering prayers of gratitude, praise, or petition, or by writing a note of comfort and support to someone who comes to mind during your prayer.

Above all, let these reflections be an invitation to encounter God in your experience. I am convinced that God wants to be known and delights in communicating with us if we will pause long enough to listen, and if we are willing to be surprised. Our life experiences are waiting to be prayed.

Thanks

Encouragement inspires writers. So my thanks go to the people who have read my column; to the editors of my column, Mary Parlin and Marilyn Zastro; to my editor at Saint Mary's Press, Carl Koch; to Fr. Bill Graham; to my family; and to all who unknowingly have inspired my life and my writing.

Reflections

I kneel by the bed for a long time . . .

when I say night prayers with our grandchildren. They have so much to be thankful for, from parents to cookies, from birds to a sunny day.

I have been working on a similar attitude of gratitude for myself: looking at the positive, seeing the good in people, focusing on what I do have instead of what is missing. Gratitude opens my heart to reality, to goodness, to the little things I take for granted. Gratitude changes attitudes. Attitudes change behaviors. Behaviors change lives. Living gratefully can change our world.

Extending hospitality is such an ordinary gift, . . .

but did you know that hospitality was celebrated as a sacrament in the early church? Only after many centuries was the number of sacraments officially reduced to seven. The other practices became known as sacramentals.

So the next time you open the door to welcome a guest, to offer a neighbor a cup of coffee and a plate of cookies, to provide a comfortable bed for someone traveling through, or a listening ear to a friend on the phone, remember that you are celebrating an ancient sacrament.

a mother comforts her young child . . .

who is afraid to go to sleep. She prays with him and reminds him that there is nothing to be afraid of because God is with him. As she leaves, he begins to cry again. "What is wrong, son? God is with you." Her son replies, "Yeah, Mom, but I need a God with skin on."

God sent Jesus, Emmanuel, God-with-us, as a "God with skin on." Through Jesus we personally experience God's love and concern for us. God also sends us to be a "God with skin on" to those who need comfort, forgiveness, and healing.

I *sometimes so limit God . . .*

that my idea of the heavenly banquet is a combo special at a fast-food spot. Yet God is a God of abundance, not scarcity. God's love for us is always a jumbo portion. Refills of forgiveness are available whenever we ask.

In Jesus, God gives us abundance. Loaves and fishes continue to be multiplied as people are fed, spiritually and physically, through the generosity of the many who serve in our congregations and communities. Glory be to God whose "power at work within us is able to accomplish abundantly far more than all we can ask or imagine" (Ephesians 3:20). God serves on fine china, not from brown bags.

*M*oses was a master excuse maker.

In the Exodus story (3:10—4:13), Moses gives God all kinds of excuses as to why he is the wrong one to lead the people out of Egypt. First he mentions unworthiness: "'Who am I that I should go to Pharaoh?'" Next he uses his lack of credentials: "'If they ask me who sent me, what am I to say?'" Then he asks: "'Suppose they won't believe me?'" His last resort is to point to his lack of gifts: "'I am slow of speech.'"

Have we used these same excuses when God or a sister or brother has called us to serve the community in some way? The God who calls us will empower us, just as God empowered Moses.

$\mathcal{D}$*id you ever wonder* . . .

how your obituary might read? Alfred Nobel, the founder of the Nobel Peace Prize, was horrified when his obituary was inadvertently printed before his death. It remembered him as the inventor of dynamite. This incident provided the occasion of his personal conversion. Instead of continuing as a merchant of death, he devoted the rest of his life to works of peace and human development (based on Bausch, *Storytelling*, pp. 61–62).

Conversion is seeing our life written up, as Nobel's was, and realizing we want it to be written differently. Conversion always points us in a new direction toward God.

We find it difficult to believe that our presence is enough . . .

when we are called to be with someone who is hurting, ill, or dying. We worry about what to do and, especially, what to say.

And yet, when Jesus faced his own agony in the garden, all he asked of his good friends Peter, James, and John was to "'remain here, and stay awake with me'" (Matthew 26:38). He did not ask them to inspire, explain, or say anything. Jesus just asked them to be with him. Presence was what Jesus wanted. Presence, even silence, is sometimes the best gift that we can give another person.

I am such a bundle of contradictions.

On any given day I am both generous and selfish, hostile and loving, forgiving and resentful, lustful and temperate, accepting and judgmental, trusting and suspicious, and lazy and productive. With Saint Paul in Romans 7:15, I cry out, "'I do not understand my own actions. For I do not do what I want, but I do the very thing I hate.'"

"Either-or" thinking has plagued me all my life. I am coming to accept that a "both-and" approach to life is healthy as well as holy. I am both saint and sinner. God accepts these contradictions in me. Can I?

One of my images of God that needs healing . . .

is God as scorekeeper. God is not databased, keeping a large spreadsheet with debit and credit accounts of my life. I won't wait at heaven's gate until the final printout is released. Unfortunately, I am my own scorekeeper, hoping my good deeds make points with God and somehow balance out my sinfulness.

I cannot earn God's love. Salvation is a gift: God's love freely given. "God so loved the world" that God sent Jesus to save us (John 3:16). God is lover, not scorekeeper.

This month marks the eighteenth anniversary . . .

of my brother Bill's suicide. Our family still experiences the pain, anger, and guilt of this complicated grief. We know that we cannot cause or prevent another person's actions, yet the "If only . . ." questions persist. Bill was not blessed with the insight of another friend: "I realized suicide was a permanent fix to a temporary problem and changed my mind."

Gone are the days when Catholics who commit suicide cannot be buried with full Catholic rites and in a Catholic cemetery. Our pastor ministered to us with care, compassion, and a beautiful liturgy of the Resurrection. Still, the special grief lingers, waiting for full healing. And the mystery . . .

Years ago, a wise woman encouraged me, . . .

"Pray as you can, Peg, not as you can't." I was frustrated by trying to be a contemplative with three children under age five. If I set my alarm for an early morning prayer time, so did one of my children. And they always seemed extra restless during good sermons.

I hear the same lament from sick people who are too weak to pray, from the depressed who lack the wherewithal to begin prayer, and from the grief-stricken who feel abandoned by God. Prayer is simply being aware of God's presence in the reality of our life, and responding in any way we can. God's mercy embraces our limitations unconditionally. Wanting to pray is to pray.

Friends: what wonderful gifts from God!

I need these women and men for support, encouragement, prayer, honesty, celebration, grieving, and inspiration. "And Jesus took Peter, James, and John . . ." (Matthew 17:1). Jesus also needed close friends in his life. He reached out for support by asking these three to accompany him as he healed the daughter of Jairus (Mark 5:37). They shared a secret with him at the Transfiguration (Matthew 17:9). He asked them to share his grief in the garden before his death (Matthew 26:37).

Jesus models for us the importance of allowing friends into our life.

a *late night phone call* . . .

about my aunt's death reminded me of our reconciliation process fifteen years ago. None of my siblings knew what caused the rift between my father and his sisters, but for twenty-five years there had been no contact between our families. One day I decided that their conflict had nothing to do with me. I wrote Dad's sisters, asking if we could get acquainted.

These gracious aunts welcomed me with open arms. We spent the first of several afternoons exploring family history, sharing pictures, and starting the relationship we wanted. "[God] . . . has given us the ministry of reconciliation" (2 Corinthians 5:18).

I learned a valuable lesson . . .

from a violet's leaf. I grew impatient to see
signs of a new plant sprouting. "Nothing is
happening," I said to myself. I pulled the leaf
out of the soil, only to discover an intricate
root system and a delicate bud, previously
invisible to my eyes.

That is how God works in my life. I wait
for a prayer to be answered or new personal
growth to take place. In my impatience I take
matters into my own hands, only to discover
God has been working all along, but under-
ground, in ways I could not see. God's timing
is perfect, not mine. It is a lesson I must learn
again and again.

a *friend and I have enjoyed some humor . . .*

over her early convent discipline called "custody of the eyes." Letting her eyes drift to anything or anyone who might distract her from God was a transgression to be confessed at chapter meetings.

Though this discipline might seem extreme and archaic, I practiced custody of the eyes myself when I turned off the television as the media stalked the suspect in a murder case. Violence assaults my spirit. Too much violence shuts me down emotionally. I am responsible for what my eyes take in, and I am responsible to protect the gift of God's Spirit within me. Custody of the eyes can be self-defense of the soul.

The Acts of the Apostles (5:1–11) tell . . .

how Ananias and Sapphira sold their farm, intending to give the proceeds to the church, but then held some back for themselves. They did not trust that God would provide enough for them in their old age. The story shows both of them struck dead for this deceit—harsh treatment, it seems. After all, they gave most of their wealth.

Even so, believing that we can control the future and trying to ensure our security can destroy life. We can become a prisoner of our fears. Perhaps it is not what a person gives that expresses his or her generosity, but what one keeps. To sort out what we need and what is extra takes radical honesty that only God's grace can give.

Have you ever seen a statue or holy card . . .

of Mary pictured as a middle-aged woman? Probably not. But Mary was not always the young woman typically portrayed. When Jesus died, she was in her late forties or older. One role ended, but her role as Mother of the church began.

We can only surmise from the faith-filled life that she led that she was an inspiration and source of wisdom to the early church. The witness of her life would encourage others to say yes in their obedience to God. We can see a beauty and a strength about Mary as an elder, a wisdom figure that can inspire all of us.

*O*n an ordinary Saturday morning . . .

an old friend and I just happened to connect. This chance visit witnessed to the truth of these words written by Caryll Houselander: "Yet it is really through ordinary human life and the things of every hour of every day that union with God comes about" (*The Reed of God,* p. 8).

During our conversation, I mentioned that a bleak housing market had yielded nothing for my returning son and his family, despite persistent prayer and searching. As we caught up on each other's lives, she happened to recall an unlisted house. It turned out to be perfect. Once again I was reminded to be open to God's surprises as I live each day.

*P*eople who are ill or in crisis . . .

often express that they experience a spiritual and emotional paralysis and are unable to pray when they need God the most. This is when the Christian community can come to the rescue, just as it did for the paralytic in Luke 5:17–20. Friends carried the paralytic and lowered him through the roof of the house where Jesus was staying. Seeing the faith of the paralytic and his friends, Jesus healed the man.

In the Bible, a person without a name represents each of us. We, like the paralytic, are sometimes unable to reach out to Christ. We need friends whose love and prayers carry us to Jesus. Sometimes we need to be those friends for others. And sometimes we can be the healing touch of Jesus.

*B*ring back the saints!

Our spirits are hungry for the stirring stories of the lives of this "cloud of witnesses" who inspire us to keep our eyes fixed on Jesus (Hebrews 12:1–2). The church has given us wonderful models of faith in the lives of holy women and men. They remained committed to the truth even in the face of death; they spoke up about injustices; they served poor people; and they lived ordinary lives in extra-ordinary ways.

Television and other media often seem to canonize less than desirable people. For the benefit of our children and our own faith, we need to include the lives of the saints in our reading to them and in our own reading.

*W*ildflowers *just let life happen.*

Jesus declared, "'Consider the lilies of the field, how they grow; they neither toil nor spin'" (Matthew 6:28). Beautiful flowers nestled in close to a stream or dotting our prairies do not strive to be beautiful and hardy. God made them so, and sustains them.

Working and spinning remind me of my striving, my driving effort to do things right, to be a perfect Christian, wife, mother, friend, employee, and writer. Instead, God invites me to relax and be a wildflower. Why is it so hard to just be, to let go, to depend on God's sustaining goodness?

Moses escaped death . . .

because two obscure and gutsy midwives, Shiphrah and Puah, disobeyed Pharaoh's order to kill all Hebrew male babies. They outwitted Pharaoh, saying, "The Hebrew women . . . give birth before the midwife comes to them" (Exodus 1:19). God blessed the midwives for guarding life.

Throughout the Scriptures, God is pictured as a midwife. Midwives help bring to birth. Surely God brought me to birth physically and spiritually. Others have been midwives in my life, too: family, friends, authors, clergy, and counselors who have assisted and encouraged my birthing process of becoming whole and holy. Thank you, men and women—midwives to my soul. Who are your midwives?

Patients often describe illness . . .

and hospitalization as a "wake-up call" to a new life. Illness helps them refocus priorities and consider changes they need to make to bring about an improved life.

Advent is a wake-up call from the church to arise from our slumber and prepare for a new life by giving our full attention to Christ, who longs to come into our midst. Purple vestments, Advent wreaths, and readings from the Hebrew Scriptures invite us to concentrate on our faith priorities as we wait for Jesus. I believe that each of us has a special Advent wake-up call.

In the stillness of the night, . . .

I could clearly hear the rhythmic pattern of the waves breaking on the shore. I felt as if God was saying, "I bring you my love again and again. My love is as constant as the waves." Unfortunately, stilling the noise of our hectic life, taking time for a retreat, getting up before the family to take some quiet time with God, all seem impossible.

Like imperceptible radio waves, God constantly sends out signals. We don't always turn on the radio of our soul. If we do, God will speak messages of peace and love to us. Often all I can do is acknowledge God's presence in the moments I have while chopping vegetables for stir-fry, waiting in the checkout line, driving somewhere alone, during any moments that I can find. Happily, God's love is constant.

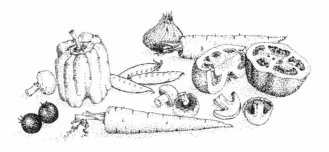

We *don't talk much anymore about our bodies* . . .

being temples of the Holy Spirit, but this truth is one of the miracles and messages of Christmas. Jesus graced our humanity by taking on a human nature, by becoming one of us. Think of it.

Think of what God enfleshed means. Our humanity is good. Our bodies are holy. To live this truth is to reverence our bodies by the choices we make regarding food, drink, sex, work, exercise, and rest. Good care of my "temple" has become a moral issue for me and a way of celebrating the Incarnation.

$\mathcal{T}$*wo young adults, . . .*

ages twenty and twenty-two, quit school to come home and provide nursing care for their mother during the last five weeks of her life. When complimented on their generosity, they responded, "We had a good teacher." Their mother had modeled courage for them, facing the adversities of her life with faith and willingness. Her service and generosity were extraordinary. Her joy lifted everyone's spirits. The Gospel their mother lived became their own.

"[Parents] are the first to pass on the faith to their children. . . . By word and example they form them to a Christian and apostolic life" ("Decree on the Apostolate of Lay People," no. 11).

I *looked into the brown eyes* . . .

of my mom's neighbor and saw a glow that I sensed could come only from a deep center. The radiance deepened as she shared her story. Helen had survived six years in a Nazi concentration camp before coming to the United States with what remained of her family. This deep pain in her life paralleled her deep faith in God and her gratitude for all that God had done for her.

Her life witnesses to the truth of Ecclesiastes 7:3: "Sorrow is better than laughter, for by sadness of countenance the heart is made glad." It is not that God wants us to suffer, but suffering can carve a certain beauty and wisdom in our heart that nothing else can.

I enjoyed my morning coffee . . .

as I marveled at the changing colors of dawn. Once again the sun rose over the horizon and cast a golden beam to me across the shimmering lake.

I was reminded in this moment that the love of God is as faithful as a sunrise. I can count on God's love. Even if a day or a season in my life is overcast, God's love is still above that cloud. "The steadfast love of [God] never ceases, [God's] mercies never come to an end; they are new every morning; great is your faithfulness" (Lamentations 3:22–23). Yes, the sunrise is a good prayer symbol to begin my day.

Deep spiritual wisdom resides . . .

in a teenager's remark, "Pain brought me closer to God." Pain has been called the megaphone of God. Pain grabs our attention. We listen up. We draw close, it is hoped, to God.

God does not cause pain. Pain is not a punishment but a part of being human, a part of life. "We know that all things work together for good for those who love God, who are called according to his purpose" (Romans 8:28). Pain can draw us to God's embrace. It can help us value the gifts that God gives us, like the beauty of creation, friends, and family. No one wants pain, but all things, even pain, can "work together for good" as we allow God's grace to work in us.

a *set of resignation papers* . . .

arrived in my spiritual mailbox. I realized God was offering me an opportunity to let go of my self-appointed role as God's chief administrative assistant.

At times I live with the delusion that I am in charge; that it is my efforts, my prayers, my worrying that holds up this world and saves all its people. God clearly states in Isaiah 45:5: "'I am the Lord, and there is no other; besides me there is no god.'" Not me. Not you. God is not an ineffectual CEO. God's wisdom and love are without match. I can let go of my need to control life, and listen to what God has in store. Well, I hope I can let go.

𝒥 flew over Nebraska . . .

on the blackest of nights. In the darkness, the beaming light of one farmhouse cast a warm glow, illuminating the entire area. I was reminded of the prologue of John's Gospel: "The light shines in the darkness, and the darkness did not overcome it" (John 1:5).

Sometimes I feel overcome by the darkness that appears in the media and by the hardships of life. I try to remember God's promise that the light will overcome the darkness. Jesus is that light, illuminating the darkness. We are called to be a light in the lives of others, shining with a warm glow of hope and support for them.

*A*n angel visiting . . .

and asking her to turn her world upside down by becoming the mother of God had to be cataclysmic for Mary. She knew that she could be socially ostracized or even stoned to death. Her "fiat" took great strength, faith, and character. "Annunciations" happen in our own lives when the unexpected shatters life as we know it. We lose our job. Serious illness strikes. A loved one is transferred overseas. We, like Mary, are "much perplexed by [these] words" (Luke 1:29).

Like Mary, our only consolation often comes from faith that God's favor is with us. As we ponder in our hearts God's promise of faithful love and Mary's shattering experience, we can hopefully embrace the strength of Mary.

Popular tunes on a fifties tape . . .

trigger my memories of friends, proms, and even a broken leg. Reminiscing gives a glow to my spirit. I realize how rich my life has been. I have celebrated good times and survived sad times. I sense, in a deeper way, the meaning of my life.

Research shows that reminiscing is a valuable process, especially in the lives of our elders. They have much to tell and few people who wish to listen. A great gift to our elders and to ourselves is drawing these wonderful stories out of them. They are often stories of faith. Reach out to an older relative or a nursing home resident. Prime the pump with "Tell me about . . ." Be sure to allow at least an hour!

*B*ecoming aware of a burglar . . .

outside our bedroom door paralyzed me momentarily, until I thought of the safety of our daughter in the next room. I was flooded with love for her and knew I was willing to die rather than have harm come to her. This love empowered me to scream. The burglar ran.

While praying several weeks later, I felt Christ remind me, "Remember how you felt when you realized you loved Rachel enough to die for her? That's how I feel about you. I loved you enough to die for you." Experiencing that Jesus loves each of us enough to die for us is what Good Friday is all about. I hope the reminder of Good Friday stays with me each day.

*B*lame *the sitcoms, . . .*

the popularity of negative humor, and the growing disdain for authority for the destructive speech patterns of our culture. We Christians have been affected. Our words can put down rather than honor, tear down rather than encourage.

Jesus took a different tack on speech. He said: "'The good person out of the good treasure of the heart produces good. . . . It is out of the abundance of the heart that the mouth speaks'" (Luke 6:45). Maybe if I start speaking about the good treasures of life, the fullness in my heart when I consider my family, the simple beauty of sunrises, I will begin to encounter even more goodness. I would like to go out of this life having planted seeds of goodness.

*G*ive the women credit . . .

for their courage in being the first at the tomb of Jesus on Easter morning. Give the men credit for believing the women's story of the risen Christ and for coming to the tomb to see. All were freed by the Spirit to step beyond the confines of their culture.

In my experience, women and men are being freed from gender boundaries by giving credit where credit is due. Relationships are gradually approaching equality, collegiality, respect, fairness, and empowerment. It is good news. Once again the wisdom of the Spirit works in us. Let's give ourselves credit for listening and responding.

*N*ow God is not a dealer; . . .

life is not a game of pinochle. But sometimes it seems as though we are dealt no aces, only losing cards. We are not being treated like kings or queens in the shuffle of life. When I feel this way, God's encouragement in Jeremiah 29:11 gets me out of self-pity: "'For surely I know the plans I have for you, . . . plans for your welfare and not for harm, to give you a future with hope.'"

Our spiritual vision is often myopic. We cannot see the whole picture. We do not understand how trials fashion us in holiness and strength of character. God always wants good for us, and suffers with us in our trials. I have to remember to invite God into my troubles. They may not magically go away, but God's presence can give strength and hope.

"*Yahweh, how many are the works . . .*

you have created, / arranging everything in wisdom!" (Psalm 104:24). Recently, I've been reading the *Book of Nature* and seeing God on every page.

Resurrected life comes forth, after a long winter, in a new budding kaleidoscope of greens, yellows, purples, and reds. Each sunrise reminds me of the faithfulness of God. The morning breeze is the breath of the Spirit. Birds greet the dawn with song, and I join in praising my God. "Glory forever to you, Yahweh! / May you find joy in your creation" (104:31).

a hunter rebuked Saint Anthony . . .

for relaxing with his disciples. Anthony responded, "Bend your bow and shoot an arrow." Repeatedly he gave this command until the hunter complained, "If I keep my bow always stretched, it will break." Anthony replied, "If we push ourselves beyond measure, we will break" (based on Bausch, *Storytelling*, p. 85).

Healthy are we if we take a day off and encourage others to do the same. Holy are we if we take some quiet time each day with God. Happy are we if we play and do something creative. Serene are we if we accept personal limitations. Wise are we if we follow Anthony's counsel.

*M*ary *lived our life.*

She knew the challenges of obedience to God, the joy of giving birth, the difficulties of family life, the sadness of losing a child and a spouse, the uncertainty of giving up one's home or country, the confusion of not understanding the path of life a child takes, the hardship of long journeys, the courage of speaking up or remaining silent, the heartache of being misunderstood, the mystery of God's way, the necessity of giving oneself for others, and the peace of following Christ.

Mary, mother to us all, pray for us. Be our guide. Be our *compañera,* our companion in life.

Our grandchildren never tire . . .

of playing hide-and-seek. Jimmy outwitted me recently, and I gave up the search. "Oma, you gave up too soon. If you would have kept on looking, I know you would have found me." Jimmy echoes a similar message from Jeremiah 29:13, "'When you search for me, you will find me; if you seek me with all your heart.'"

At times, God seems to hide from us. Prayer is dry. If God hears our prayers, God does not seem to answer them. The temptation is to give up on God. In times like this, we will find God when we ponder and ask for the graces of our baptism and hang on to God's promise of faithfulness.

Let any gossip or idle talk die within you.

"Be brave, it will not make you burst!" (Sirach 19:10). The word of God is so graphic. We all know the temptation to gossip and have given in to it. Did it help? No. Gossiping usually makes us feel worse, not better—not to mention what it does to other people.

Confidentiality is an important virtue. We could pledge ourself to seal our lips like the seal of confession. Confidentiality is a high sign of love and respect for another. We can choose to hold our confidences and to help our friends when they forget to hold theirs. And for all those times when we failed in charity by gossiping, we can attempt to make amends.

*"**D**o not abandon old friends, . . .*

for new ones cannot equal them" (Sirach 9:10). One of the gifts of having old friends is the history we have together. We have weathered toddlers and teens, and celebrated key birthdays and anniversaries. We have packed moving boxes and shared meals. We can count on one another's support.

We gathered recently with old friends whose child had just died. This sad time was softened as we reminisced about all the ways we had shared life over our thirty-year friendship. Each memory was an important thread God had woven into a lasting tapestry of friendship. Thank you, God, for old friends.

Change is right up there with mosquitoes . . .

on my "least favorite" list. Change stretches me, often uncomfortably. It throws my emotions into flux. I am invited to let go of the known and comfortable, and trust the Spirit. Furthermore, God seldom asks for my opinion about change.

This was the turbulence in my heart the day the clergy changes were announced. I felt sad about saying good-bye to a wonderful pastor who had been an inspiration and a true support. Yet I knew God was giving us another gift in our new pastor. I need God's grace to view changes with the eyes of faith and with an open heart.

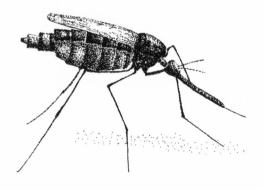

"*Marriages are made in heaven, but . . .*

so are thunder and lightning," chuckled a friend as she shared her stories about the joys and the storms she and her husband had experienced in their forty-five years of marriage.

My husband John and I laugh at the illusion of eternal bliss with which we entered marriage many years ago. Some of the "thunder and lightning" in our relationship has been our desire to hold on to self-will and unrealistic expectations, those selfish tendencies that make a lot of noise and rob us of the unity God intends for us. The grace of marriage is there for the asking, because God is a faithful partner in our covenant. I am not sure any marriage could hold together without God's grace.

With love and compassion Jesus ministered . . .

to sick people, preached to the crowds, taught in the Temple, welcomed sinners and outcasts, comforted the afflicted, called for justice, encouraged the downtrodden, gathered the children, trained apostles, forgave sins, taught others how to pray, and broke bread with many.

All Christians are called to dedicate their life in some way to this rich and diversified ministry. A shortage of professional ministers can be a blessing in disguise if it calls all of us to ministry.

𝓘 was afraid as I said good-bye . . .

to our son when he left for Guatemala to
attend a language school. Recent political
unrest there only magnified those free-
floating concerns that ranged from "Will
he return?" to "Did he take enough under-
wear?"

My head knows the truth of Philippians
4:6: "Do not worry about anything, but in
everything . . . let your requests be made
known to God." But today my parent heart
needs comforting. I need to drop my mask of
bravery and come before God and others just
as I am. I need to accept my humanness and
let God's grace transform me into the person
of trust I want to be.

I felt sad and mad . . .

as an Operation Rescue spokesperson shook his finger at a crowd, declaring that the floods plaguing the Midwest were a sign of the judgment of God on our country because of abortion. I rebelled inside. Flooding is a natural disaster, not the vengeance of God. Perpetuating the image of God as one who punishes us rather than as one who loves us unconditionally does our faith enormous harm. We live in fear of a God who sends floods on the innocent as well as on sinners. We interpret any adverse circumstance as God getting back at us, and we clutch the hope that our good deeds outweigh our bad deeds on the scales at judgment.

Jesus called God "Abba" (Daddy), hardly the ogre suggested by this man.

*H*ug *those babies; . . .*

gaze attentively into their eyes, parents, grandparents, and caregivers, because you are planting those initial seeds of faith that are crucial for life. Research on faith development shows that the quality of relationships and care in the first year of life either builds a basic sense of trust or one of mistrust in self, others, and one's environment.

We can move into a mature trust in God with greater ease if our early relationships are trustworthy and attentive. We will believe God's loving gaze toward us because it resembles that of our parents. So again, hug those babies.

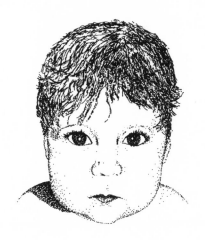

Our new grandsons . . .

remind me that my self-worth lies in who I am, not in what I do. We regard Zachary and Philip as the greatest treasures in the world. Yet they only sleep and smile, eat and void, hardly great accomplishments.

As we age, we tend to base our self-worth increasingly on what we do. Aging, illness, unemployment, or any situation that limits our productivity invites us back to the profound truth that our value lies in who we are, not in what we do. We are human *beings,* not human *doers.* We are worthwhile because we were made by God and called by name to be God's children.

*Y*ou know the game.

Friends call from the interstate, hoping to stop for a short visit. With the voice and stride of a commanding officer, you move the troops through the house so it is in spit-shine readiness when your guests ring the doorbell.

If God gave us five minutes notice before a visit, would we be just as busy cleaning our spiritual house? What would we choose to hide or clean up before God arrived? Why would we hide anything? God loves and accepts us just as we are. It's not that we shouldn't clean up our act, but God's presence transforms our trash into treasures.

I woke up this morning . . .

not wanting to be a wife or mother, not wanting to fix breakfast or go to work. As my day progressed I began to wonder if others shared my experience. Was it hard for our priest to get up for early Mass or the carrier to be prompt with the newspaper? Did the sanitation people, grocery clerk, postal worker, or my dentist want to be at their places of business today to serve me?

I realized again that this world keeps going because others do not live by whim, but keep one foot moving ahead of the other as best they can. God, keep me going, and give me a grateful heart for the services other people provide for me.

*H*aste makes . . .

waste, especially when colliding with a chair leg results in a broken toe. I sense the frustrations caused by physical handicaps. No more walks or wearing regular shoes. I cannot do what others do. I said no to reading at church today because I felt embarrassed by my limping. I faced the anger at myself and at my body for failing me.

I try to reframe the experiences of my life according to Romans 8:28, "We know that all things work together for good for those who love God." Really some good has come: I have a greater understanding of the impact of handicaps in life. I am reminded to slow down.

The Book of Proverbs claims, . . .

"A cheerful heart is a good medicine, but a downcast spirit dries up the bones" (17:22). What if laughter and a light heart are as saintly in God's eyes as prayers and good works?

When I get into my serious mode, I focus on myself, and I lack gratitude. I act as though all of life depends on me. I do not witness to the joy of Christ being my strength. A light spirit lifts everything and everyone. God must have a sense of humor to stay in love with us saints-in-the-making.

"*We brought nothing into the world, . . .*

so that we can take nothing out of it" (1 Timothy 6:7). This verse brought back a poignant memory of my father's death. As I walked out of the nursing home carrying all his earthly possessions in one cardboard box, I thought, "Well, Daddy, it isn't much to show for an entire life, but you saved the best part, your faith in Jesus Christ."

None of our earthly achievements and accumulated possessions matter at death. We take one possession into eternity: our relationship with God. The God who is love is the pearl of great price.

My heart softens . . .

as I look at the infant Jesus in our nativity crèche. I am reminded that Jesus chose to be vulnerable when he came among us as a human being. He did not shield himself from hurt, pain, doubt, risk, rejection, or being misunderstood. Rather, he opened himself up again and again to loving others.

To be like Jesus is to be vulnerable. Accepting this truth has been a life-changing experience for me. When I drop my armor and defenses, I discover the miracle of the Incarnation. "Your eternal Word has taken upon himself our human weakness, giving our mortal nature immortal value" (*The Roman Missal,* p. 382).

The next time you light a fire . . .

for a barbecue, think about the significance
of fire in the life of Saint Peter. Before Jesus'
trial and death, while sitting around a fire in
a courtyard, Peter denied Jesus three times:
"I don't know him." After the Resurrection,
Peter professed his love for Jesus at a fire by
the sea: "Yes, you know I love you."

Peter publicly professed repentance
through love. So can we. Whenever you perform this ordinary act of lighting charcoal,
let it be a celebration of your coming back
to Christ after sin.

My car never stops at garage sales, . . .

but I participated in one after reading this Scripture passage:

> "I will pull down my barns and build larger ones, and there I will store all my grain and my goods. And I will say to my soul, 'Soul, you have ample goods laid up for many years; relax, eat, drink, be merry.'" (Luke 12:18–19)

Even with the children moving out, the closets in our big, old home were full. Many things were easy to let go of, but then, without any warning, I would want to hang on to something trivial, such as a piece of jewelry or a trinket not used in fifteen years. Letting go is a complex but freeing experience. I could apply this process to other areas of my life.

I change compulsions regularly.

For a while I compulsively bought material I found on sale. When I stopped sewing I had collected a large dresser of unused goods. Of late it has been books. Someone might think I was well read to look at our bookshelves, until I admit I haven't read half of them. For a while ordering only one book at a time helped.

I blame my recent extravagance on the enticing offers in the extra catalogs that arrive in the mail. I bargained with God, "But God, the books are mostly about you." Somewhere God answered, "My child, a compulsion is always just that." With God's help I will read, not buy, this year.

*W*e opened the door of our house . . .

to a relative stranger, a cancer patient need-
ing a place to stay while he wrapped up his
affairs. This Advent angel opened our hearts
to the coming of Christ.

Jim knew darkness before coming into
the marvelous light of God's love. Jim knew
God sent Jesus into the world so that he might
be forgiven, live in freedom, and enjoy eternal life. Jim knew that with God nothing can
shake us, not even terminal cancer. "'Listen!
I am standing at the door, knocking; if you
hear my voice and open the door, I will come
in to you and eat with you, and you with me'"
(Revelation 3:20).

a holiday fashion magazine . . .

featured a sleek model and this quote from, supposedly, Julian of Norwich to entice readers to purchase an expensive black velour lounging outfit: "A cheerful giver does not count the cost of what he gives."

Julian was a fourteenth-century mystic who encouraged our total response to the generous, unfailing love of God. I doubt that giving a black velour lounging outfit was what she intended by her wisdom. This advertising ploy highlights the dishonesty of lifting any statement, even Bible verses, out of context to prove or justify one's position. It can be a dangerous misrepresentation of the truth.

a fat cardinal . . .

swooped toward our cabin, banged against the window, dropped down, and flew back to a branch, only to repeat its attack, crash, and retreat numerous times. "That bird is insane," I declared to my husband, John.

Indeed, insanity has been defined as doing the same thing over and over again and expecting different results. But I have the choice to do something different. I can change behaviors. I can avoid stress by not procrastinating until the very last minute. I can stop reacting to the behavior of another. I can keep my serenity by not trying to control a situation at work. New behaviors offer the possibility of different results—and sanity! Otherwise, I'm just a kamikaze cardinal.

*"**H**abit is habit, and not to be flung out of the window. . . ,*

but coaxed down-stairs a step at a time," wrote Mark Twain (*Mark Twain: Mississippi Writings,* p. 946). Is that why Lent is a forty-day season of conversion?

One Ash Wednesday I resolved to throw out my critical spirit. It did not work. My critical spirit kept showing up unexpectedly. I was looking for perfection rather than progress, the easy fix instead of the necessary discipline and surrender. My willingness enables God's grace to bring about conversion, one day at a time, one step at a time. It does not matter how long or how steep the staircase.

*N*ine school chums . . .

gathered for our annual reunion. Some shared stories of great joy and celebration: a promising job, a book published, new grandchildren, risks taken, a benign tumor. The mosaic of our lives also included painful, stretching times. We had been asked to accept a divorce, the loss of a child, a lesbian daughter's uncertainty, and the trauma of childhood sexual abuse.

When I gazed at the resilient, faith-filled faces of my friends, the words of Christ to the mystic Julian of Norwich came to mind: "I will make all things well; and you will see yourself that every kind of thing will be well" (*Julian of Norwich: Showings,* p. 229). Then I praised God for the inspiring strength of my friends.

*"**I** feel as if I were the guardian . . .*

of a precious slice of life, with all the responsibility that entails. There are moments when I feel like giving up or giving in but I soon rally again and do my duty as I see it: to keep the spark of life inside me ablaze." (*An Interrupted Life*, p. 195)

These words of Etty Hillesum remind me to treasure the complex gift of life. Etty died at Auschwitz. Her journal chronicles her radical trust in God and her tenacious celebration of life while she had it. I express my gratitude to God, asking God for the grace to live fully, to reverence my body, mind, and spirit with good care. With God's grace I want to "keep the spark of life inside me ablaze." No one else can do this for me.

My friend Ann grabbed an aerosol can . . .

of shaving cream and wrote in gigantic letters across their wide bathroom mirror, "The battle is the Lord's" (1 Samuel 17:47). It was her act of surrender after an exasperating day with the children.

In our effort to be good parents, we sometimes waste precious energy. We escalate friction by trying to control the lives of our children. We make everything from homework to haircuts our domain. John and I found we had to pick our battles. Even then, by letting go and relying on God, by laying down our weapons, the best victory was our inner peace.

*"**W**hat return can I make to Yahweh . . .*

for all your goodness to me?" (Psalm 116:12).
The Psalmist asks a very important question.
God has given me everything from the air I
breathe to my ability to feel.

My return will be to write a gratitude list
or "blessings of the day" list and add to it
every day: begin or increase prayer time; if I
am not accustomed to tithing, I can start
with 1 percent and build up; I might give
back my talents and time to serve my parish
in some manner; I can care for others. If my
life in faith is to be complete, I need to show
my gratitude to the loving God who showers
me with goodness.

Cancer destroyed Rosie's earthly tent, . . .

but could not conquer her indomitable spirit. She beat the odds of her life expectancy. Her dedication to faith, family, and friends deepened. The jaunty style and humor with which she faced her cancer helped others feel comfortable around her. Her hospitality and service remained constant. She accepted life on life's terms. With grace and dignity she let go of her independence, and opened up to receive the care of others.

Her life convinced me that "I can do all things through [Christ] who strengthens me" (Philippians 4:13).

I often wonder why . . .

we seem more adept and faithful in making the Lenten stations of the cross than the Easter stations of joy. During the Easter season our spirits could be exploding with the good news that Jesus Christ is risen. Easter shows us that love has conquered hate and death.

My Easter faith ought to shine with joy, peace, strength, power, excitement, hope, newness, and love. Good Friday is the necessary prelude to Easter Sunday's Resurrection and to our joy. Without the Resurrection we would be terrible fools. As Saint Paul says, "If Christ has not been raised, your faith is futile" (1 Corinthians 15:17). I want to be an alive Easter person!

"We need to take the tears . . .

we shed for Jesus and use them to wash the bloodstained faces of the Good Friday people of our own day," writes Sheila Cassidy, a British hospice physician (*Good Friday People,* p. 96). Jesus encourages the daughters of Jerusalem to do the same (Luke 23:28).

My Good Friday people include a friend facing embezzlement charges, someone who is alone, a grief-stricken priest, an abused young adult, a parent who struggles with a child's decision, an unemployed man, and a friend trying to make a new life for herself. With the energy of the risen Christ flowing in us, we can wash the faces of humanity with compassion, acceptance, and service. Who are your Good Friday people?

I *think it was Thomas Jefferson who*
said something like, . . .

"If we are too busy to have enough time
to exercise and relax early in our lives, we
should set aside a comparable amount of
time later in our lives to be ill because it
will just about even out."

Vacations need not be expensive or
lengthy or even involve travel. They simply
need to help us enter that state of relaxation
that helps rest our body and recreate our
spirit. Jesus withdrew to a quiet place. The
Creator rested on the seventh day to enjoy
the wonders of the universe. If God needed
one day off, we need at least one, too.

*B*arrenness has a beauty . . .

not readily noticeable. The western Nebraska landscape spoke to me of sameness and flatness with none of the color and lushness that tantalizes the eye. But then at some point I began to notice the beauty of each tree, each swelling of the earth silhouetted in sharp contrast against the horizon.

Our spiritual life includes barren periods and dark nights. We can fail to see the beauty of this experience. But God promises, "'I will now allure her, and bring her into the wilderness, and speak tenderly to her'" (Hosea 2:14). Often only in emptiness, devoid of distraction, can we see clearly the beauty of God's presence.

*P*onder your hands . . .

for a moment or two. Hands bless, serve, and communicate intimacy. They labor to provide for the needs of family. Hands write, love, encourage, and comfort. Hands perform surgery, fix hair, dial for help, create quilts, knead bread, diaper babies, build houses, plant flowers, make music, crochet afghans, figure taxes, bathe the elderly, paint masterpieces, and click cameras.

God uses our hands to continue creating and healing our world. Let's celebrate our hands.

***W**hen Marilyn's name appeared . . .*

on the list of classmates unaccounted for as our fortieth reunion approached, I revealed that she had died of a brain tumor shortly after graduation. Fear of Marilyn's periodic epileptic episodes had caused some in our class to avoid her. When a group of us had lined up a blind date for her for our senior prom, word got back to us that certain girls were upset. An epileptic seizure at prom might spoil their evening. But Marilyn's date was fun; her corsage was lovely.

Some months later at her wake, Marilyn's parents dressed their only child in her blue tulle formal because the prom was the happiest night of her life. Having reached out to her all those years before is still one of my most cherished memories.

Our neighborhood has bonded . . .

in a new way with the addition of bird feeders in our front yard. We share antics of the birds and squirrels as they jockey for position. My neighbors remind me to replenish the feeders. Occasionally a resplendent scarlet cardinal visits us, but usually the ordinary sparrow inhabits our perches and nestles in our bushes for the night.

As I sit at our kitchen table and watch them gather, I reflect on Jesus' words, "'Do not be afraid; you are of more value than many sparrows'" (Luke 12:7). I am that sparrow, kept by God's love.

My boat is launched.

My line is baited and cast. As I look out across the water, it is a perfect moment to reflect on the old fisherman's prayer, "Dear God, be good to me. The sea is so wide, and my boat is so small" (Le Tord, ed., *Peace on Earth*, p. 38).

What an appropriate way to approach prayer: to acknowledge the bigness of God and my smallness as a creature. What an emotional and spiritual relief to trust the wisdom, counsel, and love of God instead of depending on self and self-will. My vision is often myopic. Only God knows the whole picture, the great sea. Only the bounty of God's grace keeps my small boat safe and on course.

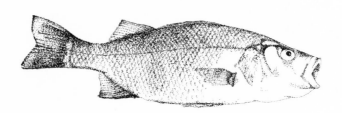

*N*ot *knowing what to say . . .*

can keep us from reaching out to a grieving person. Of Job's friends, "no one spoke a word to him, for they saw that his suffering was very great" (Job 2:13). They gave him the gift of presence. Then a need surfaced in them, as in all of us, to make sense of suffering. Rationally, with questions and accusations, they blamed Job for his troubles.

"I'm so sorry." "I'm praying for you." Simple heart statements that show care are always appropriate. And maybe an embrace or a gentle, consoling touch. Not head answers like "It was God's will" or "You can have another baby." Easy answers such as these short-circuit the grieving process and deny the profundity of our pain.

"We read to know we are not alone" . . .

is a line C. S. Lewis says in the movie *Shadowlands.* Growing up as a shy child, my books were my friends. Even now I am reminded that I am not alone in my faith journey as I read the Scriptures. Abraham let go of security to follow the call of God. Paul had his own thorn in the flesh. Mary suffered for and with her child. The Apostles were slow to grasp a new reality of church. Jesus was persecuted for what he believed. Thomas doubted. Martha kept too busy.

This "cloud of witnesses" accompanies us as we "run with perseverance the race that is set before us" (Hebrews 12:1). We are not alone.

I recently joined the "Tooth Brush Gang."

This group of people commits themselves to praying for their pastors every time they brush their teeth. Imagine a ministry that has no dues or meetings, is flexible, open to both genders, cross-generational, and multicultural!

Our pastors have the awesome responsibility of listening to the Spirit as they minister to the needs of our diverse congregations. In Colossians 4:3, Paul begs the church to "pray for us as well." I invite everyone to join the Tooth Brush Gang in prayer each morning and night.

"At the lowest place in my life . . .

I remembered the Hail Mary, taught to me
so many years ago by my grandmother,"
explained a patient.

Traditional, memorized prayers are
important in my prayer life, too. They are
comfortable and familiar connections to
God. They are communal, uniting me with
others in my faith tradition. Jesus too made
use of traditional prayer forms. He prayed
the Psalms. He also taught a new prayer, the
Lord's Prayer. What I learn from Jesus and
from this patient reminds me to respect all
manner of prayer and to value the place that
traditional prayers have in strengthening our
faith.

As a divorced woman in the 1950s, . . .

my mother did not experience acceptance and support from her church. In fact, her pastor threatened her with excommunication. Slowly over the years, we, as church, saw the injustice of such attitudes. We realized that divorced people need acceptance and care from faith communities. We try to give it.

Gay and lesbian people are a minority in the 1990s who often experience exclusion, judgment, and even violence from their Christian brothers and sisters. No one was excluded from the love and ministry of Jesus. Paul says that nothing "will be able to separate us from the love of God" (Romans 8:39). I pray for such love among us.

$\mathcal{T}$wo aging locksmiths . . .

treated our grandson as their most important customer of the day. They patiently fitted keys and looked up a lost combination. "Take good care of your lock collection, young man," the owner remarked as we left.

True grandmother that I am, I recognized this as a teachable moment. Driving home, we talked about the men's courtesy, patience, encouragement, and obvious joy in helping him. I am convinced that faith and values for life are caught, not taught. Those two locksmiths showed my grandson how to "do to others as you would have them do to you" (Luke 6:31).

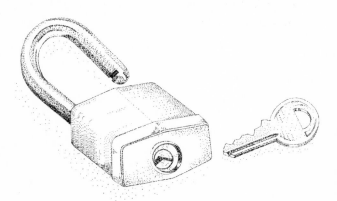

The life of Martha . . .

reminds me to keep a balance between doing and being, to be a prayerful person attentively listening to God, and to live the gift of hospitality.

Jesus chides her, "'Martha, Martha, you are worried and distracted by many things'" (Luke 10:41). Another facet of Martha that strikes me is that she seems too concerned about how her sister lives her life. This tendency to control another comes out in my Martha voice, "Wouldn't it be better if . . . ?" "Why don't you . . . ?" "I can't understand why she . . ." Better to focus on my own behavior.

Lately, while rereading . . .

our friend Dan's letters from Vietnam, I had the incredible awareness that our love helped keep him alive during that war. God's grace carried the love of his friends across a vast country and ocean, reminding him that he had something to live for and someone to come home to.

The poet Emily Dickinson writes, "Love is the Fellow of the Resurrection / Scooping up the Dust and chanting 'Live'!" (Thomas H. Johnson, ed., *The Poems of Emily Dickinson*). Loving each other heals, encourages, and strengthens. It gives and sustains life.

"*One hundred years from now, . . .*

it will not matter what your bank account was, the sort of house you lived in, or the kind of car you drove—but the world may be different because you were deeply involved in the life of a child." (Anonymous)

We believe in and want to make this difference as parents. Yet many pressures in our life pull us away from family. We need to take an honest inventory occasionally, accepting the things we cannot change, but having the courage to change the things we can, for stronger families.

*B*ecause *of my husband John's job,* . . .

we have always lived away from our relatives. We are grateful to the many friends who pinch-hit and become family for holidays, baptisms, and overall support.

An African proverb says, "It takes the whole village to raise a child." The nuclear family, often on the move, is hard-pressed today to handle the rigors of raising children. We can find ways to reach out as neighbors, coworkers, foster grandparents, aunts and uncles, and as parish communities to become extended family to help support the children and their parent or parents.

*A*dvent celebrates . . .

the experience of waiting in our lives. We wait for our prayers to be answered, for a job, for hurts or grief to be healed, for reconciliation with a child, for news from the doctor, for babies to be born, for good weather, for recovery from surgery, for company to arrive, or for depression to be lifted.

"O Lord, be gracious to us; we wait for you. Be our arm every morning, our salvation in the time of trouble" (Isaiah 33:2). Our ancestors waited with expectant faith. Give us the grace, God, to do the same.

*O*n Ash Wednesday, . . .

I usually stand poised for my Lenten tri-
athlon of fasting, prayer, and good works,
concerned about whether I will have the
endurance to complete the forty days. I wonder if this athletic spirituality really fits the
spirit of Lent.

   In order to enter into the paschal mystery, the dying and rising of Jesus, I need to
be concerned about emptying not achieving,
less not more, God's grace rather than my
efforts, being grasped by God not striving for
God. Approaching Lent this way would
transform my resolutions and me.

My debut behind a lawn mower . . .

produced more sweat than nice, even rows. It isn't that mowing was beyond me or below me, but by habit I've concentrated on inside chores.

Today one son and I compete for baking the best sweet rolls. Another son tackles a dress shirt with deft sweeps of the iron. A daughter is budget-perfect. A new paradigm is emerging in many households, including ours, that promotes collaboration, working together. Jobs are shared according to needs, schedules, and talents, rather than gender. It is a respectful, creative process.

𝒩o other family in the county . . .

had to live by such extreme guidelines, complained our children during their years growing up. John and I spent time and prayer
creating a vision that we hoped was God's
will for our family, a concept beyond their
shortsighted view.

I notice now as our children begin their
own families that they search for this same
vision, even if this means making choices
that are counter-cultural or unpopular. Deep
down, I believe that we all realize parents are
ultimately responsible to God, as well as to
their children, for the decisions they make.

𝓘 recently met a priest . . .

who lives the sacrament of the Eucharist in a most challenging way. His home, a three-story row house in the slums of Philadelphia, is a haven for the black neighborhood youth who need a bed, a meal, an advocate, a listening ear, or a father figure to relate to. His life inspires me to live the sacrament of the Eucharist in a more conscious way: to be open to being blessed, broken, and given for love of others.

We live the Eucharist all week long as we care for our children or an elderly parent, or when we go the extra mile for someone in need.

J meet incredibly generous people . . .

who care for their parents, take over their parents' business affairs, and make adjustments in their own schedules to provide help, visits, and transportation. Some take their elderly parents into their homes. Often these new responsibilities come at the time in their life when they have envisioned a season of freedom and independence for themselves.

From the cross, Jesus asked his disciple John to take care of his mother Mary, and "from that hour the disciple took her into his own home" (John 19:27). I have frequently wondered what wisdom John would have for those who continue this ministry. From the Gospel and Epistles attributed to him, John would certainly have told us to love. I wish I knew more specifics though.

Hope, that beautiful Christian virtue, . . .

takes us out of ourselves and our circumstances into possibility, courage, and creative waiting for God's timetable. Hope accepts questions without answers, the night with only the promise of dawn. The song of hope can be sung only because we believe God has promised to be faithful to us and has only our good at heart.

Together with the Psalmist we pray, "For you alone are my hope. / Yahweh, I have trusted you since my youth; / I have leaned on you since I was born" (Psalm 71:5–6).

$\mathcal{D}$*ear Mary Magdalene, . . .*

You are a favorite faith model because you
loved Jesus so extravagantly. Sometimes I am
so cautious, stingy, and reserved. You never
counted the cost, pouring expensive oint-
ment and washing his feet with your tears.
Your only focus was loving Jesus, not what
the others at table thought of you. Sinner
though you were, you knew God's forgiveness and perfect love for you.

   Did gratitude for the new life that Jesus
gave you liberate you? Did joy well up within
you so that you could not contain it? Mary,
my mentor and friend.

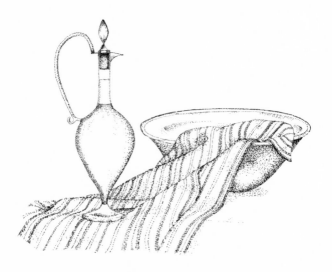

*M*any Catholic priests, sisters, and brothers . . .

take vows of poverty, chastity, and obedience. Karl Rahner, a famous German Jesuit theologian who died in 1984, remarked that all of us take these vows when we die: poverty because we take nothing with us, chastity because we die alone, and obedience because we can no longer sin anyway.

Perhaps if we integrated these vows into our manner of living we would be better prepared to die. Living simply, nurturing solitude and silence, and following God's will give our life harmony, balance, and readiness for meeting God in the next life.

*O*ur diocese welcomed . . .

several hundred men and women into the church at the Easter Vigil. The great joy and celebration was heard in every parish.

We trust one of the reasons our newcomers were attracted to our church was that they saw us as a loving community, living out the command of Jesus: "I give you a new commandment, that you love one another. . . . By this everyone will know that you are my disciples, if you have love for one another" (John 13:34–35). Jesus' commandment is simple yet so difficult. To keep it, I have to examine myself with a question like, Would other people recognize me as a Christian by the way I love others, my kind speech, courtesy at work, and willing service to my neighbor?

How can our "Big Mac-, . . .

TV tray-style-of-dining" generation ever be able to understand the Eucharist as a special meal, a ritual banquet? In the Eucharist, we take time to be together as the family of God, receiving Christ as our food and drink. We bring gifts, ourselves, and some monetary contribution. We set a table with a fine cloth, candles, flowers, and special dishes. People prepare celebrative music, readings, and a homily. Sometimes we even dress up.

We make this fuss to celebrate the gift of Jesus to us. We receive the food we need for our journey in faith. If we seldom or never celebrate special meals together at home, will we lose our appreciation for the Eucharist and our capacity to be nourished by it?

𝒯he pregnancy of our daughter-in-law . . .

one Advent was the focus of my faith journey. For me, Lisa modeled Mary, the Theotokos "God-bearer," the one who brought Christ into the world through the willing openness of her life.

Mary was what we are all called to be: Christ-bearers. We incarnate God in our barren world through our love, through the fruit of our life as we live out the Gospel. When Christmas finally came, I asked: How does Christ want to be born anew in my life? How can I be God-with-us—Emmanuel?

"Vegging in the Valley" . . .

is the title of the latest movie script I wrote for my life. I run a one-woman operation with my name listed as scriptwriter, leading actor, producer, and director. As the film rolls, the script has changed. God's name is in lights, not mine!

People frequently comment that their life did not turn out as planned. It is difficult to accept that we are not in control of the universe, much less our life. I'm slow to trust God's wisdom "for my thoughts are not [God's] thoughts, nor are [God's] ways my ways" (Isaiah 55:8).

My New Year's prayer is borrowed . . .

from a friend, "God, help me to be the kind of person my dog thinks I am." Daisy considers me faultless, guiltless, and moodless. Oh, that gift of unconditional love, complete with wagging tail, so freely given by the canine species!

God's gift of unconditional love empowers me to be my best self, to love myself and others. God's welcome and acceptance of me is not based on whether I deserve it or not. God sees the good in me, sees what I am becoming. If I saw me as God sees me, my life would change immeasurably. For now I pray that this may come to pass.

"*It's a great thing . . .*

to be on a journey into the unknown, particularly when you trust the cabbie," wrote a missionary from Chile (Cassidy, *Good Friday People*, p. 69). Remembering this verse helped me get over my anxiety as I rode through a dangerous part of Philadelphia. The priest I was with was well loved in this community, so we were safe.

God as cabbie might seem disrespectful, almost sacrilegious. And yet there is no safer experience than to get out of the driver's seat and let God drive through the hazardous streets of life.

Saint Paul . . .

gives us an inspirational yet practical course in good parenting. In 1 Corinthians 13:4–7,13, he says, and I paraphrase:

> Love will enable us to be patient and kind through interrupted schedules and toddler two's. When we are wrong, we will admit this. We will not discipline in anger, nor keep score with our teenagers. When parenting is difficult, we will remember that there is no limit to love's forbearance, to its trust, hope, or power to endure.

> Of all the gifts we give our children, the greatest, and perhaps the costliest, is love.

𝓘 noted at dinner one night . . .

how social conversations, as well as the media, increasingly focus on our fear of violence, vandalism, and the unknown. As we named those fears, Jim suggested that the real culprit is not out there, outside ourselves, but rather in the unnamed fears within ourselves. I realized that my deepest fear is that God cannot be attentive to all my needs and those of my family.

John declared, "Perfect love casts out fear" (1 John 4:18). I have a hard time understanding, let alone making, a radical surrender to God, completely depending on God for my well-being and that of my loved ones. Again, I pray, hope, and wait for such love.

*P*assing the buck.

Blaming. Finding a scapegoat. Justifying. Making excuses. Not taking responsibility for our actions. Adam blamed Eve, and Eve blamed the serpent. We've been blaming ever since.

"You make me . . . ," "But . . . ," "I forgot because . . . ," "If you would only . . . ."—all these send up red flags in my conversations, reminding me that I am blaming someone else. This behavior is neither honest nor responsible. It disrupts my relationships. God calls me to be accountable. Adam and Eve did not fool God. I doubt if I do either. God, help me stop trying to.

"*If some miracle of healing would happen, . . .*

I'd win. If I would die and go to heaven, I'd win. It's a win-win situation no matter how I look at it." A young mother with cancer paraphrased these words of Paul in Philippians 1:20. Paul wrote them from prison, conveying his ambivalence about living or dying. He wished only that Christ would be exalted in both.

My dying friend and Paul: two giants of faith living twenty centuries apart! Firm faith in Christ makes us winners no matter what. I would hate to think what dying slowly of cancer would be like without such faith and hope.

In *"Cry, the Beloved Country,"* . . .

one of Alan Paton's characters remarks, "'The tragedy is not that things are broken. The tragedy is that they are not mended again'" (p. 25).

The tragedy is not that people are sick. The tragedy is that so many have no insurance for proper care. Old age is not a tragedy, but loneliness that is not mended by simple acts of kindness and companionship is a tragedy. A death may not be tragic, but leaving a friend unconsoled is a tragedy. Pregnancy is not a tragedy, but ignoring a woman with no support creates a tragic situation. Christ calls us to be menders of hearts and repairers of social systems, not writers of tragedies.

For a meditative half hour, . . .

I lay on the hard cot in the Red Cross Center.
After a history of anemia, I had finally been
accepted to donate blood. As I watched my
blood drip into the marked bag, I thought
about Jesus on the cross, shedding his blood
that we might have life and healing. A pint is
not much to give, considering that Jesus gave
his life for us.

As the nurse carried away my blood, I
prayed for the person who would receive this
transfusion. I hoped it would help heal or
maybe even save a life. Would that healing
the soul could be so tangible.

*D*ogs bark . . .

at whatever they don't know. So do people. How easy it is to growl out of ignorance at another person, another group, changes in the church, a different way of believing or living. I am slow to get to know someone else, to hear their story, to study, to ask for an explanation, to allow for differences. I find myself opting for simple, effortless answers that pamper my ego.

A mentor once challenged me, "There isn't a person you could not love, Peg, once you've heard his or her story." This has been my experience and my growth. So, these days, I try to bark less than I used to.

Organization has never been my strong suit.

Too often I am scurrying around when family members arrive home rather than giving them the welcome they deserve. People are kept waiting while I frantically search for a lost file. Being organized allows time for the important things. More than anything I want to make our home a place that facilitates our common life together, where calm and order add to the quality of our relationships.

What needs to happen here? is a valuable question for a family conference, a process that allows mutual input and accountability. Over the years, I wish that I had asked this question more often around our house.

*C*onjugating Latin verbs . . .

with Sister Charlotte Ann had few perks, but one lasting gift of our two years together is the awareness of the root meaning of many English words. I might call a close friend a good companion and describe how I enjoy his or her company. Companion and company come from the same root word, *companio: com*, meaning "together" or "with," plus *panis*, meaning "bread."

Companions share many kinds of bread together: the bread of their lives, dreams, needs, wants, disappointments, joys, and sorrows of living. We share the bread of our life with only a treasured few companions. I always find such sharing nourishment for my heart, mind, soul, and body.

Acknowledgments *(continued)*

All other scriptural quotations in this book are from the New Revised Standard Version of the Bible. Copyright © 1989 by the Division of Christian Education of the National Council of the Churches of Christ in the United States of America. Used with permission. All rights reserved.

The excerpts on pages 14 and 47 by William J. Bausch are from *Storytelling: Imagination and Faith* (Mystic, CT: Twenty-Third Publications, 1984), pages 61–62 and 85. Copyright © 1984 by William J. Bausch. Reprinted with permission. Published by Twenty-Third Publications, P.O. Box 180, Mystic, CT 06355; toll-free: 1-800-321-0411 (paper, 232 pp., $7.95). Further reproduction without permission is prohibited.

The excerpt by Caryll Houselander on page 26 is from *The Reed of God* (New York: Sheed and Ward, 1954), page 8. Copyright © 1944 by Sheed and Ward.

The excerpt on page 34 is from *Vatican Council II: The Conciliar and Post Conciliar Documents,* "Decree on the Apostolate of Lay People," no. 11, Austin Flannery, ed. (Northport, NY: Costello Publishing Co., 1980), page 778. Copyright © 1975 by Harry J. Costello and Rev. Austin Flannery, O.P.

The excerpt on page 64 from the song "Christmas III" is from the English translation of *The Roman Missal* (New York: Catholic Book Publishing Co., 1985), page 382. Copyright © 1973 by the International Committee on English in the Liturgy. All rights reserved. Used with permission.

The excerpt on page 71 is from *Mark Twain: Mississippi Writings,* selections by Guy Cardwell (New York: Viking Press, 1982), page 946. Volume arrangement, notes, and chronology copyright © 1982 by Literary Classics of the United States.

The excerpt by Julian of Norwich on page 72 is from *Julian of Norwich: Showings*, translated by Edmund Colledge and James Walsh (New York: Paulist Press, 1978), page 229. Copyright © 1978 by the Missionary Society of Saint Paul the Apostle in the State of New York.

The excerpt on page 73 is from *An Interrupted Life: The Diaries of Etty Hillesum, 1941–1943* (New York: Washington Square Press, 1985), page 195. Copyright © 1981 by De Haan/Uniebock b.v., Bussum. English translation copyright © 1983 by Jonathan Cape.

The excerpts on pages 78 and 109 are from *Good Friday People*, by Sheila Cassidy (Maryknoll, NY: Orbis Books, 1991), pages 96 and 69. Copyright © 1991 by Sheila Cassidy.

The excerpt on page 84 is from *Peace on Earth: A Book of Prayers from Around the World*, edited by Bijou Le Tord (New York: Delacorte Press, 1992), page 38. Collection, adaptations, and illustrations copyright © 1992 by Bijou Le Tord. Used by permission of Delacorte Press, a division of Bantam Doubleday Dell Publishing Group.

The excerpt by Emily Dickinson on page 92 is from *The Poems of Emily Dickinson*, Thomas H. Johnson, ed. (Cambridge, MA: The Belknap Press of Harvard University Press). Copyright © 1951, 1955, 1979, 1983 by the President and Fellows of Harvard College. Reprinted by permission of the publishers and the Trustees of Amherst College.

The excerpt on page 114 is from *Cry, the Beloved Country*, by Alan Paton (New York: Charles Scribner's Sons, 1948), page 25. Copyright © 1948 by Alan Paton.